The Original
M. J. Beagle Guide

THE
NEW HAMPSHIRE
PRIMER

WITH SPECIAL SECTIONS FOR CANDIDATES, INCLUDING:

-- WHY N.H. HOSTS THE FIRST-IN-THE-NATION PRIMARY

-- HOW NEW HAMPSHIRE'S FRANKLIN PIERCE
GOT ELECTED PRESIDENT <u>WITHOUT REALLY TRYING</u>

-- A <u>STEP BY STEP GUIDE</u> AND <u>MONEY-BACK GUARANTEE</u> *
THAT YOU'LL <u>WIN</u> THE PRIMARY !

* Double the book price back if you do lose !
Keep the book free, and try again in four years !

Other Fine Books
from
Moose Country Press

Sit Free or Die — M. J. Beagle
John Stark, Clear Thinking, Daniel Webster,
and New Hampshire's Outhouse Heritage

A Country Life — William S. Morse

The Big Fish of Barston Falls — Jack Noon

The
New Hampshire
Primer

The
New Hampshire
Primer

by M. J. Beagle

Moose Country Press
Warner, N.H.

ISBN 0-9642213-4-9

Library of Congress Cataloging-in-Publication Data

Beagle. M. J. (Moosilaukee Jack)
    The New Hampshire primer / by M.J. Beagle.
        p.   cm.
    ISBN 0-9642213-4-9 (perfect bind. : alk. paper) : $9.95
    1. Presidents--United States--Election--Humor. 2. Primaries--New Hampshire--Humor. 3. Presidential candidates--New Hampshire--Humor. 4. New Hampshire--Politics and government--Humor.   I. Title.
E176.1.B32   1995   95-5387
973'.099--dc20   CIP

10 9 8 7 6 5 4 3 2 1
Printed in the United States of America

DEDICATION

To the memory of
Franklin Pierce

Native son of New Hampshire.
President of the United States,
1853-57.

The nicest guy
and handsomest man
ever to be President.

Franklin Pierce

Contents

Author's Foreword

Illustrations

Harper's Magazine
Heart of the White Mountains, Samuel Adams Drake, 1882
Leslie's Monthly
Library of Congress
Life of Gen. Frank. Pierce -- The Granite Statesman, C.E Sester, 1852
Life of Gen. Frank. Pierce of New Hampshire, D.W. Bartlett, 1852
Messages & Papers of the Presidents, J.D. Richardson, 1897
Mount Washington in Winter, 1871
National Handbook of American Progress, E.O Haven, 1876
Natural History of Animals, Sanborn Tenney, 1875
Ned Nevins -- The Newsboy, Henry Morgan, 1867
Scribner's Monthly
Vanity Fair

Grateful Acknowledgement is expressed for permission to reproduce
the Franklin Pierce silhouette from the Bowdoin College archives,
and for excerpts from the 1852 campaign cartoons from the
Dartmouth College Special Collections.

AUTHOR'S FOREWORD

have occasionally been accused of being an overly sensitive, canine sentimentalist. Some say I can't take criticism -- perhaps it's true. I never have liked being in the limelight, and, quite frankly, I've been reluctant to write this book.

The last time I wrote a book* as a public service, I got blasted by the very chuckleheads I was trying to lead from ignorance and reform into useful citizens. They didn't appreciate it.

Chucklehead politicians took offense at my observation that some politicians sought "elective office as a combination of sanctuary and feeding trough."

Chucklehead historians were upset when I pointed out that there were history-improvers among them "... who, though they don't make much of a mark on the present, manage more readily to nudge the past towards the way it should have been ... to make history serve the present better and be more entertaining."

I failed to get the Bunker Hill monument and the Bennington monument moved.

I have yet to see anyone follow my advice and achieve the greatness of John Stark and Daniel Webster.

Why then should I bother again to write a book as a public service?

Well, partly because over the years the New Hampshire primary has grown to be an important early step in the selection of the president of the United States. My writings might make a difference in getting the right sort of candidate nominated and elected. Despite the recent attempts at "primary poaching" by other states, it is quite apparent that "As New Hampshire goes, so goes the nation" (and everybody else, if they know what's good for them). But without a proper understanding of what makes New Hampshire tick, the electioneering hopefuls are likely to go hopelessly astray.

---

* *Sit Free or Die: John Stark, Clear Thinking, Daniel Webster, and New Hampshire's Outhouse Heritage*; M. J. Beagle, Moose Country Press, 1994

1

Though I myself am certainly qualified to be president (natural born citizen, at least thirty-five years old, at least fourteen years[†] a resident of the United States), I am not now, nor will I likely ever be, in the running for the office of president of the United States. I would refuse the nomination if it were offered. Neither do I have any personal stake in a possible role as political king-maker or queen-maker. I don't expect a *quid pro quo* ambassadorship, a cushy job in the White House, or a political appointment in New Hampshire. I wouldn't even take one of those nice post office jobs if it were offered.

There are other reasons why I should bother to write another book -- old fashioned reasons intended for the good of our great country:

- Because it's New Hampshire -- threatened, but not yet over-whelmed by the neon and noise of the flashing, cackling, American mono-culture. New Hampshire -- a place where clear thinking about the past, present, and future is still possible. New Hampshire -- one of the few states left with the potential to form a candidate into a better national leader.

- Because New Hampshire produced John Stark and Daniel Webster, and both of them would have bothered to help our country get the right kind of leadership. It's time our nation had another leader of their caliber.

- Because I've always had a soft spot for the underdog candidate who is the right sort of person. I can't stand seeing good people get beaten time and again by low-life, run-of-the-mill, chucklehead politicians.

- Because the more time a candidate spends traveling around New Hampshire looking and listening -- studying the state's great heritage -- the better person he or she will be, and the better president.

- And finally, because New Hampshire's Franklin Pierce knew exactly how to be elected president, *and I know just how he did it.*

M. J. Beagle

[†] Based on the conversion ratio of one to seven for an equivalence of canine to human years -- still awaiting a test case to take before the United States Supreme Court.

Part I

An Unofficial History of the N.H. Primary

A BRIEF HISTORY OF THE
NEW HAMPSHIRE PRIMARY

n Franklin Pierce's day and for many years afterwards there was no New Hampshire presidential primary. The prominent leaders of various established political parties in the state -- Whig, Democratic, Republican -- and of other ephemeral ones -- Know-Nothing, Free-Soil, and the like -- decided among themselves who they would send as delegates to their parties' national conventions. These delegates, through their voting at the conventions, selected the candidates for president.

In 1910 New Hampshire eased into the primary process -- the first New England state to do so -- but only for selecting candidates for state offices. Under the new system the popular vote rather than the party bosses decided who the candidates would be.

A few years later the state voted in as law a bill to select delegates to the national presidential conventions, also by popular vote. The bill set the date for this change in the New Hampshire political process for the third Tuesday in May of 1916.

After this bill had passed, the 1915 state legislature took a closer look at it. Traditional town meeting day had always been the second Tuesday in March -- a good use of a day in mud season.

Town residents had long been in the habit of talking over their local issues then and voting on them. It seemed pretty silly to the 1915 legislators to require New Hampshire voters to gather at their town halls twice in just a little over two months. Why not save a trip? Common sense prevailed. Town meeting day and primary day were combined to use up jointly a day in mud season.

On that second Tuesday in March of 1916 New Hampshire's primary was held the same day as Minnesota's. Indiana's primary had been a week earlier. Four years later, however, Indiana had changed its primary day to May, and Minnesota had dropped its primary completely. It was in 1920, the same year that the ratification of our constitution's nineteenth amendment gave **women the right to vote,** that New Hampshire held its *first* first-in-the-nation presidential primary. And it has continued to hold the country's earliest presidential primary ever since.

For three decades, New Hampshire's primary selected delegates to the national party conventions in what was essentially a popularity contest among the state's political figures. These politicians wanted the prestige of going to their parties' national conventions as delegates. Once they got there, they would officially pick the nominee.

New Hampshire voters sometimes had the chance to vote for delegates pledged to a particular candidate, but that was as close as they got to picking a presidential nominee. The fact that the New Hampshire primary came earlier than all the others was no big deal, and reporters from outside the state didn't pay any attention to it.

In 1949 the New Hampshire Legislature revised the primary law so that it became, in effect, a presidential preference poll.

Things really started to change in 1952, the first year that New Hampshire voters started choosing delegates who were all pledged to specific candidates for president. Dwight Eisenhower had retired from his heroic military career and was then president of Columbia University. Eisenhower enthusiasts in the state who thought he'd make a good Republican president for the United States decided that they would show him, by the results of the New Hampshire primary, that he had enough support to be the country's president if he wanted to be. They actively began campaigning for him against his main -- and well-qualified -- competitor, Robert Taft of Ohio. Taft supporters campaigned right back. For the first time, really, the New Hampshire primary promised to be an interesting contest. Reporters from afar began looking at it.

Just before primary day, Taft showed up in New Hampshire. With several busloads of reporters, he made a whirlwind tour of the state, actively campaigning. His tour probably earned him some votes, but he lost anyway. Taft never realized at the time just what sorts of seeds he had planted; what precedents he had set for candidates in future New Hampshire primaries.

The few out of state reporters who covered New Hampshire during the 1952 primary campaign had a wonderful vacation visiting the state: breathing the clean, cool New Hampshire winter air, frolicking in snow drifts, and meeting some of the very interesting natives of the state. Also, for the first time in history they got an inkling of the full potential of expense accounts.

7

Looking for a way to guarantee more such vacations, they wrote glowing reports of the New Hampshire primary and of how important it was. They shared secrets with other reporters and with political analysts about creative uses of expense accounts, good places to eat, and scenic spots to visit. A lot of articles and analyses about the New Hampshire primary began appearing in the national press.

Soon there was no question about how necessary it was to cover thoroughly every New Hampshire primary. Later, reporters and analysts publicized the importance of covering all the primaries thoroughly -- not just in New Hampshire, but in all the states that held them.

From just a few paltry weeks spent covering the New Hampshire primary, their working vacations mushroomed into months of enjoyment with free meals, free hotels, and free entertainment. The reporters and analysts formed symbiotic relationships with political poll takers, and everybody had a good time. Before long, political consultants, retired politicians, and a lot of out-of-work Hollywood technicians began drifting into New Hampshire during the primary campaigns looking for ways to make themselves indispensable.

Thus the presidential primary business was born. It has been a good growth industry. And it all began in New Hampshire.

N.H. 653: 8 ELECTIONS

653:9 Presidential Primary Election.

The presidential primary election shall be held on the second Tuesday in March or on the Tuesday immediately preceding the date on which any other state shall hold a similar election, whichever is earlier, of each year when a president of the United States is to be elected. Said primary shall be held in connection with the regular March town meeting or election or, if held on any other day, at a special election called by the secretary of state for that purpose.

★　　　★　　　★　　　★　　　★　　　★

HOW TO FILE AS A CANDIDATE
FOR PRESIDENT OR VICE-PRESIDENT
OF THE UNITED STATES
IN NEW HAMPSHIRE

How to File:

During the filing period, which will begin on the first Monday in December of 199– and will end on the Friday of the following week, a declaration of candidacy must be filed in the secretary of state's office along with a filing fee of $1,000. Declarations of candidacy will be available from the secretary of state's office. The information required on the declaration is as follows:

> I, _____, declare that I am domiciled in the city (or town or unincorporated place) of _____, county of _____, state of _____, and meet the qualifications for the office for which I am a candidate; that I am a registered member of the _____ party; that I am a candidate for nomination for the office of _____ to be made at the primary election to be held on the ____ day of ___; and I hereby request that my name be printed on the official primary ballot of said _____ party as a candidate for such nomination.

Signature and address of candidate is required on the declaration.

★　　　★　　　★　　　★　　　★　　　★

8462
THE STATE OF NEW HAMPSHIRE
Department of State
State House, Room 204
107 North Main Street
Concord, N. H.
03301 - 4989

Part II

Franklin Pierce

" Sometimes You Win ...

A CLOSE LOOK
AT PRESIDENT FRANKLIN PIERCE
AND AT HOW HE GOT HIMSELF
ELECTED PRESIDENT

ranklin Pierce was by far our handsomest president. No one else has even come close.

James "Old Buck" Buchanan
President 1857–1861

A comparison with Buchanan, whom some have claimed was good looking, is laughable. It's true that Buchanan had nice hair, except for that tuft that stuck up in front, but his skin was like uncooked pie-crust rolled out with a stick of firewood.

A comparison with Harding, the other most frequently mentioned contender, is an even worse joke. Harding had the posture and the skin, but his eyebrows were all wrong -- too wide and bushy -- and he could never find the right toupee to match them.

Franklin Pierce's hair was naturally perfect. Despite the disadvantages of doing without a blow-drier, a hair stylist, or modern tinting and mousse-enhancement technologies, he clearly had the best looking hair of any president before or since. All he had to do was run a comb through it half a dozen times

Warren Gamaliel Harding
President 1921–1923

each morning, and he was ready for any situation. Over his four year term in office he thus saved many hours, which he used for fighting with Congress, fishing, or just for thinking clearly.

13

His posture was inspiring. Whether he was arguing a case in a New Hampshire courtroom during his lawyer days, in his uniform for the Mexican War, or simply standing around being nice, his posture made him a man to be noticed and remembered.

His skin naturally had the golden glow of health without any need for miracle-goo, night-time applications.

And he was a pretty good dresser.

Clearly, by our modern standards he was thus *well-qualified* to be president, but in the nineteenth century, only those who personally met Franklin Pierce could be impressed properly by his good looks. The vast majority of the people who voted for him never got to see him in person and had to settle for looking at engravings that showed a fairly handsome guy, but never did him total justice. He would have gotten even more votes if people could have seen him as he was.

F. Pierce at Bowdoin College

Franklin Pierce was also the nicest guy in the world. His college friends at Bowdoin, among them Nathaniel Hawthorne and Henry Wadsworth Longfellow, always had good things to say about him. Even after he became a lawyer, everybody still thought the world of him. While he was president, the members of his cabinet liked him so well that none of them ever left; thus making Pierce the only president to go through his term of office without a single cabinet change. He accomplished this stability with cabinet members from all over the United States at a time of increasing sectional divisions, which eventually would lead to the Civil War.

His Secretary of War, Jefferson Davis, did a particularly thorough job enlarging and modernizing the very army his Confederacy would be battling within only a few years.

It's true that some very nasty chuckleheads in Washington said terrible things about President Pierce. That was because he refused to do things the way they wanted them done. President Pierce's job was to lead the United States; to hold the country together against the forces that were trying to tear it apart. He did his job well and made enemies of those whose policies would have destroyed the country. These enemies hated him without even knowing him. If only they'd bothered to talk with him for a few minutes, they would quickly have seen how nice he was and surely would have changed their minds and stopped their vile comments.

If people before the election of 1852 could have seen Franklin Pierce on television, he would have won in an all but unanimous land-slide. As it was, Pierce didn't need the modern technology. He captured the popular vote in twenty-seven states out of thirty-one and won the electoral vote 254 to 42.

Pierce's campaign strategy to get his party's nomination and win the election might work today, given an equally attractive candi-date, so it's important to know what it was. Here's how he got to be our fourteenth president.

Franklin Pierce began his march to the White House with twelve years of serious résumé padding to prove that he had what it took to become president and to get people to notice him, and he finished it with a decade of passive restraint. By passive restraint, I mean that he played hard to get.

His résumé included the following:

- a reputation as a consistently nice guy.
- a practice as a successful lawyer.
- election to the N.H. House of Representatives at age 24.
- election as Speaker of the N.H. House at age 26.
- election as United States Congressman at age 28.
- election as United States Senator at age 32.

His decade of passive restraint began when, after serving five years of his six year term as senator from New Hampshire, he resigned his office and returned to New Hampshire to practice law. This was an attention getting move. At a time when most senators would be throwing their re-election campaigns into high gear or else, if they weren't planning to run for re-election, quietly packing up their office furniture and getting ready to go home, Pierce took the un-usual step of resigning. Then he went home, kept quiet, and waited.

A few years later, in 1845, when Levi Woodbury of New Hampshire resigned from the U. S. Senate to become a Supreme Court Justice, Governor Steele of New Hampshire attempted to appoint Pierce to fill out the unexpired term. His fellow New Hampshire citizens noticed the offer and wondered what he would do.

Pierce declined:

"My personal wishes and purposes in 1842, when I resigned the seat in the senate were, as I supposed, so perfectly understood that I have not, for a moment, contemplated a return to public life. Without adverting to other grounds which would have much influence in forming my decision, the situation of my business, professional and otherwise, is such that it would be impossible for me to leave the state suddenly, as I should be called upon to do, and be absent for months, without sacrificing, to a certain extent, the interests, and disregarding the reasonable expectations, of those who rely upon my services."

In 1846 President Polk offered him a cabinet position as attorney general.

Pierce declined in a nice letter to the President:

"Although the early years of my manhood were devoted to public life, it was never really suited to my taste. I longed, as I am sure you must often have done, for the quiet and independence that belongs only to the private citizen, and now, at forty, I feel that desire stronger than ever.

"Coming unexpectedly, as this offer does, it would be difficult, if not impossible, to arrange the business of an extensive practice, in a manner at all satisfactory to myself, or to those who have committed their interests to my care, and who rely on my services. When I resigned my seat in the Senate in 1842, I did it with the fixed purpose never again to be voluntarily separated from my family for any considerable length of time, except at the call of my country in the time of war."

Again people noticed, and they wondered. They knew that Franklin Pierce would have done a good job in Polk's cabinet. They were somewhat gratified later in the year to see him accept appointment as United States district attorney for the state of New Hampshire, but shook their heads at the notion that he had declined the honor of serving in a president's cabinet.

GENERAL FRANKLIN PIERCE.

In 1847 he answered "the call of my country in the time of war."
In February he was appointed a colonel of infantry. By the time he
marched off to fight in the Mexican War he was a brigadier general.

We won the war. Pierce returned home to New Hampshire.

In 1848 Democrats in New Hampshire offered to nominate Pierce for governor of the state. He again declined. People again took notice.

In 1850 he was elected president of the New Hampshire Constitutional Convention -- a personal, public service. He got nearly ninety-eight per cent of the vote.

As the 1852 presidential election approached, Pierce shifted his nomination and election strategies into high gear. New Hampshire delegates wanted to put his name in nomination at the Democratic national convention to be held in Baltimore. Not wanting to appear overly eager for the office, Franklin Pierce stayed at home in New Hampshire and sent the following message to Charles G. Atherton, one of New Hampshire's delegates to the convention:

> "The same motive which induced me several years ago to retire from public life, and which since that time has controlled my judgment in this respect, now impels me to say that the use of my name, in any event, before the Democratic national convention at Baltimore, to which you are a delegate, would be utterly repugnant to my tastes and wishes."

This masterful note demonstrated just the right touch of restraint. Franklin Pierce was well on his way to clinching the nomination. Just to make sure things came out right, he sent one last note to Colonel Lally, another New Hampshire delegate.

> "As I told you, my name will not be before the convention; but I cannot help feeling that what there is to be done will be important beyond men and parties -- transcendently important to the hopes of Democratic progress and civil liberty."

Already he was talking like a president.

In June, 1852, Franklin Pierce was still at home in New Hampshire, even while the Democrats held their national convention in Baltimore. Strong delegations there pushed the candidacies of William Marcy, Stephen Douglas, Lewis Cass, James Buchanan, and others. Ballot after ballot they stubbornly held out for their favorites, and no one got enough votes to win. Had the delegates been able to meet Pierce personally at the national convention, talk to him, and compare him to their own candidates, undoubtedly the voting

GREAT FOOTRACE FOR
THE PRESIDENTIAL PURSE
{$100,000 & PICKINGS}
OVER THE <u>UNION</u> COURSE 1852.

wouldn't have gone much further than the first ballot. However, because Franklin Pierce was in New Hampshire, the delegates at the convention had to get a sense of the man second hand, and it would take forty-nine ballots before he was chosen the official Democratic party candidate for president.

The Whigs held their national convention later the same month, also in Baltimore. Horribly shaken by the challenge of finding a candidate young enough and good enough to run against Franklin Pierce, they were in complete disarray. To their everlasting shame they passed over Pierce's good friend, the aging Daniel Webster, and thus deprived the American voting public of the unique prospect of choosing between two good candidates, both sons of New Hampshire.

After a deadlock of fifty-three ballots, the Whigs' improvident solution was General Winfield Scott, a leader who had been dubbed *Old Fuss and Feathers* by the soldiers who had served under him. Oddly enough Scott had been Pierce's commanding general in the Mexican War. Perhaps the desperate Whigs had convinced themselves that he might also have a chance to outrank Pierce at the ballot box. Foolish thought.

After the Whig convention a disappointed Daniel Webster saw the handwriting on the wall. He knew that he'd missed his last chance to be president and that the American people would laugh the Whig party right out of existence for its choice of Winfield Scott to run against Franklin Pierce.

Webster would undoubtedly have voted for Franklin Pierce in the election had he lived long enough. His death in October unfortunately deprived him of the chance. Before he died, however, he conveyed a message to Pierce through Rufus Choate:

"Tell him that after the second day of November next, the Whig party, as a national party, will exist only in history."

The great Daniel Webster proved to be right. *Old Fuss and Feathers* fussed and flounced through the campaign. Franklin Pierce stayed close to home and ran his presidential campaign at a pace nearly as subdued as his campaign for the nomination. He was elected fourteenth president of the United States without a hitch. The Whig party did indeed go belly up and within a few years had faded away completely, never to be heard from again.

WINFIELD S. SCOTT
(Old Fuss & Feathers)

DANIEL WEBSTER

CAPABILITY AND

AVAILABILITY

President Franklin Pierce

... sometimes you lose. "

In 1856, four years after his election, President Pierce was denied another chance to face the voters at the polls. At the Democratic nominating convention he would be turned out to pasture by his own party despite his real accomplishments and good looks. Franklin Pierce learned that standing presidents may do their best and still fail to get re-elected despite a memorable record and a robust and growing economy. That's the way it goes. Pierce served out the rest of his term and went home to New Hampshire. The nation moved ever closer to civil war.

Regional hatreds within the country had overwhelmed even the best efforts of Franklin Pierce. And for years afterwards, Pierce was condemned by many for not solving the problems that would lead to the War Between the States. Others faulted him for not fighting the War sooner. Even after his death in 1869, his memory would be tarnished well into the 20th century by chucklehead historians and politicians who lied that Pierce did nothing as president. It's time to set the record straight.

PIERCE'S ACCOMPLISHMENTS AS PRESIDENT, 1853–57

" More than just a pretty face. "

California Gold Rush

Very early in his administration President Pierce gave his personal endorsement to the California gold rush. Without his support the Forty-Niners likely would have become bored after three or four years of looking for gold and probably would have abandoned their efforts. With his support, they stayed and kept finding enough gold to finance the brilliant future of the great state of California. We have Franklin Pierce to thank today for the fact that California is more than just a collection of mud huts.

Railroad Expansion Incentives

Pierce made farsighted investments of huge tracts of federal land by giving them to railroad entrepreneurs in exchange for having them build railroads. It didn't cost the American public even one penny to get a lot of railroads built. Pierce was sharp enough to get it done for free. The commercial lifeblood of our nation has pulsed over these arteries of steel ever since.

Gadsden Purchase & Camel Acquisition

Pierce made an awesome real estate deal with Mexico. He bought land that expanded the New Mexico territory of the United States southward. This expansion gave to the later state of Arizona its whole south end and to the later state of New Mexico its southwestern corner. Without Pierce's efforts all this land would still belong to Mexico. The entire acreage of the Gadsden Purchase has proven to be a paradise with no black flies whatsoever and very few mosquitoes. It is also an excellent source of clean fill.

As if Franklin Pierce hadn't already done enough for the future state of Arizona, he also oversaw the importation, in 1856, of thirty-four camels to work as freight haulers in the area. How many other presidents would have gone out of their way like this?

Captured Nicaragua

In 1856, General William Walker of Tennessee led an expedition which seized control of Nicaragua. President Pierce recognized the new government Walker set up, but unfortunately for Walker, the Nicaraguans drove him out of the country after six months, and he quick-stepped back to Tennessee.

PRESIDENT PIERCE'S,

March and Quick Step,

Composed and arranged for the

PIANO FORTE

Got a railroad built across Panama

This was a lot quicker and easier than the undertaking half a century later of digging a canal. By shuttling goods between the Atlantic and Pacific shipping lanes, the Panama railroad saved ships from the long and dangerous trip around the tip of South America. By building a railroad instead of a canal, President Pierce -- in these days of primitive canal safeguards -- undoubtedly kept the Atlantic Ocean from emptying into the Pacific, an environmental disaster of the worst sort.

Opened trade with Japan

In 1854 Commodore Matthew Perry negotiated a treaty with Japan that gave the United States a "most favored nation" status and brought Japan out of centuries of isolation. Typically for President Pierce, he shrugged off the praise for this accomplishment and tried to give the credit to Millard Fillmore, his predecessor, so that Fillmore would have at least something on an otherwise meager list of presidential accomplishments.

Annexation *(pretty close)* of Hawaii

In 1854 Pierce had his Secretary of State, William Marcy, negotiate a treaty of annexation with Hawaii. It was a done deal, but a wishy-washy Senate, overly swayed by British protests at this move, refused to ratify the treaty. So the Hawaiians just had to wait and wait and wait for the times to catch up to Pierce's foresight.

Purchase *(almost)* of Alaska

Pierce had Secretary Marcy offer to buy Alaska from the Russian minister if Russia were inclined to sell. The Russians thought it over for more than a decade and then decided that they would sell. We bought.

Annexation *(just about)* of Cuba

Pierce made this one of his administration's chief goals and kept trying a lot of different moves to accomplish it. Unfortunately he didn't get the legislative support. Franklin Pierce was right, of course. If representatives and senators had only followed his lead, our country would have completely avoided the headaches of the Spanish-American War and of Fidel Castro.

A century later, without access to Cuba, the United States would suffer the virtual extinction of its cigar smokers, with lasting effects on politicians at every level. Pierce was so far ahead of his time on this issue that we're still waiting.

Part III

THE M. J. BEAGLE

STEP BY STEP GUIDE

*FOR PRESIDENTIAL
CANDIDATES*

Quick question:

Would Franklin Pierce's winning strategy
be something that would work today?

Quick answer:

Yes, if you adapt it to modern conditions
and use it better than anybody else.

Quick question:

How do I do that?

Quick answer:

Start with step one.

STEP ONE

irst get yourself elected senator or representative or governor from your home state and serve one or more terms. New Hampshire voters want to see at least this minimum level of experience. While you are in office, pay close attention to your hair, your clothing, your posture, and to staying out of jail. Practice sincerity in front of a mirror for at least half an hour every day.

STEP TWO

Over the course of serving your terms of office for your home state start getting your name mentioned by others as a possible presidential contender. How you manage this is your own business, but you'll have your best chance if your name is out circulating no later than a year after the last presidential election. Plan far enough ahead so that, in the final months before the primary, the people of New Hampshire won't think of you as just another in the herd of candidates who all descend on the state at about the same time. Ease into this step. Smile significantly whenever reporters ask if you might be a candidate, but stay non-committal.

STEP THREE

Learn as much as you can about New Hampshire, her history, her heroes, and everything else that makes the New Hampshire heritage so far superior to that of all other states. Do this before you head north so that, when the opportunities come up in your frequent visits to New Hampshire, you'll make a good impression. Don't set foot in New Hampshire until you already know a lot about the state, and keep studying right up until Primary Day.

STEP FOUR:

START BUILDING YOUR CAMPAIGN ORGANIZATION

This is a critical early step. Eventually, depending on how your campaign is progressing, you may decide to hire a consulting firm to tell you what you need to believe in, what events you need to stage, and which parts of your opponents' pasts you need to reveal in order to get elected. If you succeed in finding the right people for your campaign team, however, you won't need a consulting firm. Consulting firms are very expensive and in a lot of ways are like auto mechanics. Use them when something seems to be broken or in imminent danger of breaking down. When your car is running well, it is pointless to hire an auto mechanic to ride around in it with you running up the bill. Less expensive members of your staff can probably give you much the same advice as the consultants. Newspaper files of past primaries and your own, in-house pollsters can probably give you a good idea of what you need for success in the primary. And if the people working in the consulting firms are as good as they claim to be, then why is it that none of them have ever been elected president? They couldn't have all the answers.

Line up a head fund raiser first, and give him or her a commission rather than a salary. Discretion must be used in fund raising until you formally announce your candidacy (Step Eight). Line up a campaign manager as well very soon after you've hired a fund raiser. Retired New Hampshire politicians are a good bet, and remember -- no sales tax.

32

Eventually, after you've formally announced your candidacy, you'll need to hire people to look after the various responsibilities of your campaign, but don't put them on the payroll until you have to. Set your campaign manager to work lining them up and your fund raiser to work to pay for them all. Here are a few of the critical, campaign organization positions of the past several New Hampshire primaries:

- fund raiser
- campaign manager
- pollster
- advance team manager
- head of the media manipulation team
- wardrobe consultant
- television makeup specialist
- emergency make-up repair team
- windy day hair specialist
- sincerity trainer
- insect repellent person

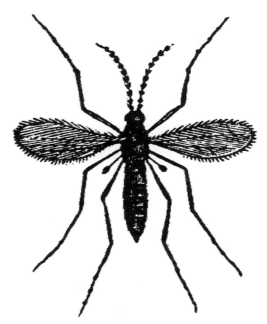

Shown Actual Size

- organizer of volunteers
- photo-op coordinator
- spontaneous events manager
- map reader/geographer
- interpreter for northern dialects

- speech writer
- speech coach
- spelling coach
- interrupter coach
  (for debates)
- negative image
  de-fuser
- crowd development
  officer
- crowd control
  officer
- slime utilization team

And don't forget your

- animal liaison officer

Use your imagination and add other specialists you'll need in order to get elected -- the more New Hampshire locals the better.

STEP FIVE:

MANAGED NEWS CONFERENCE NUMBER ONE

hough you won't officially announce your candidacy for some time yet, this step informally initiates your campaign -- ideally, three and a half years before the primary; gets New Hampshire voters to look at you differently than they do at other contenders.

Your goal here is simply to be noticed. Take this step before there are any other serious candidates in the state, and you'll get credit for originality. Those following you will just get credit for copying.

For your first managed news conference have someone tip off New Hampshire newspaper and television reporters exactly when and where you, a possible presidential contender, will be having your first lunch in the state. Make sure the reporters know that you'll be giving them a free meal. Plant someone in this free-lunch audience to ask this question:

" DO YOU HAVE PRESIDENTIAL ASPIRATIONS? "

Your answer:

> " I certainly do. That's exactly why I'm here.
> I'm going to climb every single one of them. "

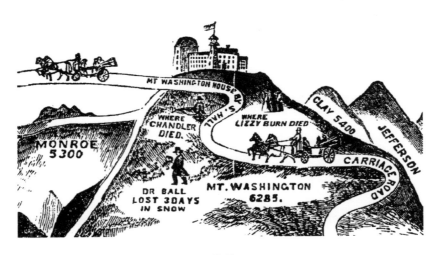

Right here is the time to launch into a brief, heartfelt speech of how long you've been wanting to take a vacation in New Hampshire and do some mountain climbing to see if the mountains of New Hampshire are as beautiful as you've heard they are.

If you want to impress the reporters far beyond the bounds of the free lunch, this is the time to recite the names of all New Hampshire's mountains that bear the names of presidents.

Memorize them and practice reciting them aloud:

- Washington
- Adams
- Jefferson
- Madison
- Monroe
- Jackson
- Pierce
- Lincoln
- Hayes
- Garfield
- Cleveland
- Big Coolidge
- Eisenhower
- North, South & Middle Carter, Carter Dome
- Clinton

Mt. Pierce, Elevation 4,310 feet

You will further impress the reporters by telling them that because you realize that Mt. Clinton's name was changed by the legislature in 1913 to Mount Pierce, you will climb that one twice.

The free lunch proves to New Hampshire reporters that you are a serious presidential contender. The mountain climbing response to the old, old question proves to them that you have a sense of humor, some originality, and will probably be fun to write about.

STEP SIX

Go climb.

Because of your conscientious attention to the duties the voters of your home state elected you to undertake, climbing all the Presidentials will require several trips to New Hampshire. Make certain that local reporters are kept well informed of your progress in fulfilling your "presidential aspirations" and that they get a few statements from you that New Hampshire's mountains are even more beautiful than you had heard. By this time the head of your media manipulation team should be on board, at least on retainer, and should start earning his or her salary by spreading the stories around nationally.

STEP SEVEN:

MANAGED NEWS CONFERENCE
NUMBER TWO

his step involves fishing on Lake Winnipesaukee, New Hampshire's largest lake. Because you are out to catch more than just fish, this news conference needs to take place during a Winnepesaukee fishing lottery. You pay money for a ticket. You get prizes according to the prize categories for big fish or for fish wearing tags. There are two such lotteries each year: an ice fishing one in the winter; a boat fishing one in the spring. An organized candidate will have time to participate in three of each over the course of three years.

Lake Winnipiseogee

Show up in Meredith for ice fishing first, and fish in the closest media-accessible spot out among the bob house village that pops up on the ice each winter.

WIND SPEED (MPH)	CHILL FACTOR (EQUIV. TEMP. ON EXPOSED FLESH)												
40	1	-4	-15	-22	-29	-36	-45	-54	-62	-69	-76	-87	-94
35	3	-4	-13	-20	-27	-35	-43	-52	-60	-67	-72	-83	-90
30	5	-2	-11	-18	-26	-33	-41	-49	-56	-63	-70	-78	-87
25	7	0	-7	-15	-22	-29	-37	-45	-52	-58	-67	-75	-83
20	12	3	-4	-9	-17	-24	-32	-40	-46	-52	-60	-68	-76
15	16	11	1	-6	-11	-18	-25	-33	-40	-45	-51	-60	-65
10	21	16	9	2	-2	-9	-15	-22	-27	-31	-38	-45	-52
AIR TEMPERATURE (°F)	35	30	25	20	15	10	5	0	-5	-10	-15	-20	-25

Because of the cold, a free lunch might not be enough to draw the reporters this time. Have an open bar as well. You need to convey to the reporters your usual small talk about how your hiking is coming along, how close you are to achieving your presidential aspirations, and how you like New Hampshire more and more with each visit.

Also make sure you are familiar with the 347 correct ways of spelling Winnepiseogee, especially important if you plan to stop at a local school for a "safe" media event later. Before hitting the lake, you should be able to identify all known species of New Hampshire fish, extinct or otherwise, and know the right bait for each.

And bring your own worms.

Your important message, however, and reason for this whole trip to New Hampshire consists of just three words:

" TESTING THE WATERS. "

New Hampshire reporters will love these three words when, three years and then two years and then one year before the primary, they hear them out on the ice of Winnypesiakee during a fishing derby.

For decades they've been sick of hearing these same old words in parking lots (with no free lunch in sight, let alone an open bar) from bumbling presidential candidates who show up and utter them as excuse or reason for visiting the state about the time that everybody in the world starts thinking about the primary. Early on you can milk this one for all it's worth. Just make sure that the reporters find out about every fishing trip you take or think about taking to New Hampshire.

Show up again after ice-out for the spring Winni derby "to test the waters" from a boat. In early summer go fishing for trout on the Androscoggin or the upper Connecticut or for horned-pout just about anywhere else "to test the waters." Keep your media manipulator and insect control crew gainfully employed. Don't forget to buy a fishing license and to obey all New Hampshire Fish & Game regulations – any infractions will invalidate the *M. J. Beagle Primary Guarantee*, and you'll also forfeit your fish.

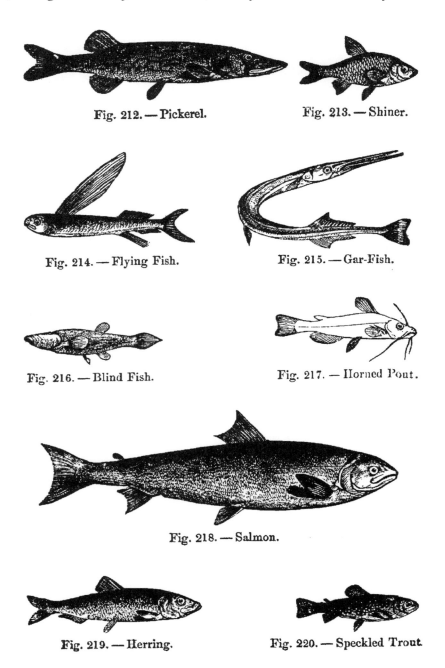

Fig. 212. — Pickerel.

Fig. 213. — Shiner.

Fig. 214. — Flying Fish.

Fig. 215. — Gar-Fish.

Fig. 216. — Blind Fish.

Fig. 217. — Horned Pout.

Fig. 218. — Salmon.

Fig. 219. — Herring.

Fig. 220. — Speckled Trout.

5ᵗʰ Mile   6ᵗʰ Mile   8ᵗʰ Mile   Recuperated

STEP EIGHT

Hold your last, and most important, managed news conference in the summer, eight months before the New Hampshire primary. This one will be on the summit of Mount Washington to celebrate your climb of the last of New Hampshire's Presidentials. There you will announce to the gathered throng that, having now climbed Mount Washington, you have achieved all of your presidential aspirations except for one:

" President of the United States. "

Mount Washington Cog Railway

Reporters this time will need free lunch, an open bar, and free tickets up and down the Mt. Washington Cog Railway, an antique train that goes right to the summit and saves a lot of steep walking.

You will also need to have both your speech writer and speech coach on board. Be well prepared to deliver a zinger of a speech on your reasons for seeking "higher" office.

Be sure to compliment reporters for the nice stories they've already written about you and make a few heart-felt comments about New Hampshire's unmatchable natural beauty. Make sure your speech writer understands all this long before you reach the top, or else read the speech before you deliver it.

If the "worst weather in America" arrives at the same time you do, quickly refer to the similar storm that greeted President Grant on his visit to Mount Washington and invite everyone inside for appropriate stimulants before you're blown into Tuckerman's Ravine.

The Flume

Chucklehead politicians may be unappreciated.

STEP NINE

At this point you have the best start of anyone. Your campaign organization is in place. The New Hampshire reporters already know you well and have gotten some good stories from you. They are certain to point you out to the national media as they begin to dribble in with the other primary candidates -- your competition.

Your media handler should be very busy by now. As you meet the voters in each of New Hampshire's six geo-political zones,[*] you need to focus on not doing anything wrong and on your appearance, behavior, and small talk. If you've hired your staff wisely, the specialists in their various areas should be able to handle any situation that comes up.

In December, go to Concord to register officially for the primary. First you'll have to find the New Hampshire State House. You can hardly miss it. Go up and down Main Street until you see a building with a big gold dome on top. That's the State House. No candidate who's ever had to ask directions to find it has ever done well in the New Hampshire primary.

Glance at the flags and portraits as you cruise the halls, but keep moving. There are only two places in the State House that you should concern yourself with. The first is the Secretary of State's office. You should go there in person to register and pay the filing fee. (Smart candidates pay the filing fee *in cash* to avoid even the slightest chance that a check might bounce -- an embarrassment for a candidate, sure death for a campaign.)

Second, locate the Governor's office. You'll want to return there later to pay your respects and pick up your free autographed picture of the Governor.

The timing of events becomes increasingly important as primary day approaches. If you haven't yet lined up enough interesting information on your opponents from your research, hire extra help now. This is not an area to try to cut costs in. Your slime utilization team should be working closely with your media manipulation team planning the various bombshells they need to drop during the debates and in the final week before the primary.

---

[*] *The Flatlander's Guide to New Hampshire*, M. J. Beagle

STEP TEN

Congratulations. Your efforts have paid off, and you've won the New Hampshire primary -- just as I promised you would. The rest, as they say, will be history.

But somebody else won the primary, too -- somebody in the other party. Both of you will need to continue on through the less important primaries in other states and then to your parties' national conventions. After that you'll likely be running against each other in the national election. Only one of you can win, but if both of you have learned the right lessons from the people you've met in New Hampshire, our country can't lose.

Don't forget those people you've talked to in New Hampshire who work hard for a living, have learned to think clearly, and aren't afraid to speak their minds. They are the bedrock of the Granite State.

Remember what they stand for, whether you win the presidency this time or next time or not at all:

- *Do your own thinking. Don't let anyone do it for you.*

- *Hard work gets a job done. Talking doesn't.*

- *Keep government small and local, and*
  don't spend money you don't have.

- *Skin your own skunks.**

- *And remember –*
  No Taxes !

Good Luck.

★　　　★　　　★　　　★　　　★　　　★

---

* *A Country Life*, William S. Morse, Moose Country Press, 1995

Printed by
Highland Press
U.S.A.

ATTENTION
ORGANIZATIONS, SCHOOLS, GROUPS

Quantity discounts are available on bulk purchases
of this book for educational purposes,
fund raising, or gift giving.
For information,
contact